The Clothing of Books

Also by Jhumpa Lahiri

In Other Words
The Lowland
Unaccustomed Earth
The Namesake
Interpreter of Maladies

The Clothing
of
Books

Jhumpa Lahiri

Translated from the Italian
by Alberto Vourvoulias-Bush

VINTAGE BOOKS

A Division of Penguin Random House LLC • New York

A VINTAGE BOOKS ORIGINAL, NOVEMBER 2016

Copyright © 2015, 2016 by Jhumpa Lahiri

All rights reserved. Published in the United States by Vintage
Books, a division of Penguin Random House LLC, New York,
and distributed in Canada by Random House Canada, a division
of Penguin Random House Canada Limited, Toronto.

Vintage and colophon are registered trademarks
of Penguin Random House LLC.

The Clothing of Books was first presented as a speech given
in Italy at Festival degli Scrittori in 2015 and subsequently
published, in slightly different form, in both English and Italian,
by the Santa Maddalena Foundation, Rosano-Firenze, in 2015.

The Library of Congress Cataloging-in-Publication Data has
been applied for.

Vintage Books Trade Paperback ISBN: 978-0-525-43275-3
eBook ISBN: 978-0-525-43276-0

www.vintagebooks.com

Printed in the United States of America
10   9   8   7   6   5   4   3   2   1

Camerado! This is no book;
Who touches this, touches a man.

Walt Whitman, *Leaves of Grass*

The Clothing of Books

1.

The Charm of the Uniform

In the house of my father's family in Calcutta, which I visited as a child, I would watch my cousins getting dressed in the mornings. They got themselves ready for school; I, on the other hand, was on vacation. They donned every morning, after bathing and before having breakfast, the same thing: a uniform.

My cousins attended different schools and therefore their respective uniforms were also different. My male cousin wore navy blue cotton pants. My female cousin, a few years older, wore a sky-blue skirt. Apart from these two colors, and the yellow tie my male cousin had to knot around his collar, the rest of the uniform was identical: a white short-sleeved shirt, white socks, black shoes.

In the closet there were surely two pairs of navy pants, two sky-blue skirts. It was enough to put on what was cleaned and pressed. In America, before leaving for India, my mother would buy several pairs of white socks, knowing that my aunt would be grateful for them.

However simple and functional, I found my cousins' uniforms splendid, fascinating. On the street, on buses and trams, I was struck by this visual language, thanks to which one could identify and classify thousands of students in such a large and populous city. Every uniform represented belonging to one school or another. Each of my peers in Calcutta enjoyed, to my eyes, a strong identity and, at the same time, a sort of anonymity. This is the effect of the uniform.

I would have liked a uniform myself. Whenever I would go to the seamstress to be fitted for new clothes—a particular adventure I could experience only in India, where, in the 1970s, it was still common to wear handmade garments instead of buying one's clothing in stores—I was tempted to ask for one. It was a foolish desire on my part. Apparel of this kind would have been of no use for me. In America I attended public school, where everyone wore what they wanted. And I was tormented by this choice, by this freedom.

When I was a child, expressing myself

through clothing was a source of anguish. I already felt different, conspicuous because of my name, my family, my appearance. In all other respects, I wanted to be just like everybody else. I dreamt of sameness, even invisibility. Instead, forced to find my own style, I felt badly dressed, the exception rather than the rule.

It didn't help that some of my classmates, finding my clothes somewhat strange, used to tease me. They would say: *What an ugly outfit. Those two things clash, didn't you know? No one wears bell-bottoms anymore, they're out of style.* They laughed. That is why, for many years, while I waited for the school bus, my day began in a state of humiliation.

My classmates derided me and, implicitly, also my parents. Being foreigners, they bought my clothes with an eye toward savings and not toward fashion or norms. They bought my clothes at end-of-season sales or at used clothing stores, knowing that I would outgrow the items in less than a year. My mother, moreover, did not share the taste of American moms. She did not shop in the same stores or dress me like the other girls. This is why I thought that a uniform would have been the solution.

Clothing has always carried additional layers of meaning for me. My mother, even today, fifty years after leaving India, wears only the traditional clothing of her country. She barely tolerated my American clothes. She did not find my jeans or T-shirts cute. When I became an adolescent, she disapproved of short skirts, high heels. The older I grew, the more it mattered to her that I, too, wear Indian or, at the very least, concealing clothing. She held out for my becoming a Bengali woman like her.

Every time we went to a party held by another Bengali family, to an important event or celebration, she would ask, implore, in the end force me to wear Indian clothing. If I protested, she would get angry. To placate her I gave in, but I would get irritated and sulk. As soon as I put on those clothes I felt like a different person, a foreigner like her. I felt the weight of an imposed identity. Those clothes, which had their own separate space in my closet, had a discordant, showy quality: colors that seemed too bright, material rooted in another land. They were, actually, more elegant than my everyday clothes, but they discomfited me. They tasted of a faraway place. They weighed almost nothing, and yet they weighed on me.

Throughout this bitter struggle between my mother and myself, of long standing and with no clear resolution, I learned the hard way that how we dress, like the language we speak and the food we eat, expresses our identity, our culture, our sense of belonging. From childhood I understood that the clothes I wore, wherever I was, rendered me an "other." Even in Calcutta, whenever I went out with my cousins, whom I physically resemble, I was perceived as a foreigner, often addressed in English. When I would ask them why, the answer was, with a shrug of the shoulders, *It must be your clothes.*

As an adult, I dress the way I want; I decide how I present myself. But the shadow of that old anxiety remains: the fear of being badly dressed, of choosing wrongly and being judged. Every so often, overwhelmed by my wardrobe, by the pressure of having to choose the right outfit, I still wonder if it would be simpler to adopt a sort of uniform.

When my books were first published, when I was thirty-two years old, I discovered that another part of me had to be dressed and presented to the world. But what is wrapped around my words—my book covers—is not of my choosing.

I am forced, at times, to accept book jackets that I dislike, that I find problematic, disappointing. I tend to give in. I say to myself, Let it go, it's not worth the battle. But I end up feeling afflicted, resentful.

What in Italian is called a *sovraccoperta* (literally, "overcover") is also called, in English, a jacket. A jacket made to measure, conceived and created specifically to cover and package a hardcover book. It should fit like a glove. And yet, in my opinion, most of my book jackets don't fit me, which is why I sometimes think, as a writer too, that a uniform would be the answer.

2.

Why a Cover?

The definition of the word *copertina* (cover) in my Italian dictionary is quite succinct: "The paper or cardboard wrapper that covers a book, notebook, or magazine." My own definition, on the other hand, is much more extensive, with other nuances, declensions.

A cover appears only when the book is finished, when it is about to come into the world. It marks the birth of the book and, therefore, the end of my creative endeavor. It confers on the book a mark of independence, a life of its own. It tells me that my work is done. So, while for the publishing house it signals the arrival of the book, for me it is a farewell.

The cover signifies that the text inside is clean, definitive. It is no longer wild, coarse, malleable. From now on the text is fixed, and yet the cover has a metamorphic function as well. It transforms the text into an object, something concrete to publish, distribute, and, in the end, sell.

If the process of writing is a dream, the book cover represents the awakening.

The news that a new cover is about to arrive elicits ambivalent emotions in me. On the one hand, I am moved because I have successfully brought a book to conclusion.

On the other hand, I fret. I know that when the cover makes its appearance the book will be read. It will be criticized, analyzed, forgotten. Even though it exists to protect my words, the arrival of the cover, linking me to the public, makes me feel vulnerable.

The cover makes me aware that the book has already been read. Because in reality, the book jacket is not only the text's first clothing but also its first interpretation—both visual and for sales promotion. It represents a collective reading by the book designer and various people at the publishing house; it matters how they see the book, what they think of it, what they want from it. I know that before a book is launched, the cover has to be discussed, considered, approved, by many.

The first time I see one of my covers, while thrilling, is always upsetting. No matter how effective or intriguing it may be, there always exists, between us, a disconnect, a disequilibrium. The cover already knows my book, while I have yet to make its acquaintance. I try to get used to it, to get close to it.

My reactions are various, visceral. Covers can make me laugh or want to cry. They depress me, they confuse me, they infuriate me. Some I can't quite figure out, they leave me perplexed. How is it possible, I ask myself, that my book has been framed in such an ugly or banal way?

The right cover is like a beautiful coat, elegant and warm, wrapping my words as they travel through the world, on their way to keep an appointment with my readers.

The wrong cover is cumbersome, suffocating. Or it is like a too-light sweater: inadequate.

A good cover is flattering. I feel myself listened to, understood.

A bad cover is like an enemy; I find it hateful.

There is a certain awful cover for one of my books that elicits in me an almost violent response. Every time I am asked to autograph that edition, I feel the impulse to rip the cover off the book.

The more I think about it, the more I am convinced that a cover is a sort of translation, that is, an interpretation of my words in another language—a visual one. It represents the text, but it isn't part of it. It can't be too literal. It has to have its own take on the book.

Like a translation, a cover can be faithful to the book, or it can be misleading. In theory, like a translation, it should be in the service of the book, but this dynamic isn't always the case. A cover can be overbearing, dominating.

Whatever the outcome, a cover imposes an intimate relationship between author and image. This is why it can lead to a sense of complete alienation. If I don't like a cover, I want to back away from it at once. But I can't. The jacket touches my words, it's wearing me.

This moment teaches me to let go of the book. It signifies a loss of control.

The cover is superficial, negligible, irrelevant with respect to the book. The cover is an essential, vital component of the book. One must accept the fact that both these sentences are true.

It always strikes me that in the "Reading" page of *Corriere della Sera*, the cover is given a grade, alongside "writing style" and "plot," in every book review. Initially I thought, It's not right. Why this level of attention? Why should the visual garb matter in judging the book? Later, I changed my mind. It makes sense. Once the cover exists it's part of the book, and has an effect, either positive or negative. It either attracts or repels the reader.

We take for granted that every book has a cover. Without one it's considered naked, incomplete, in some ways inaccessible. It lacks a door through which to enter the text. It lacks a face.

As a girl, I wrote my first "novels" in a series of notebooks. I drew a cover, therefore, for every story. I made sure that the essential elements were all there: the title of the work, the name of the author. I aimed for compelling graphics. Sometimes there was also an illustration or a portrait of the protagonist. Other times no.

Why do covers exist? First and foremost, to enclose the pages. In centuries past, when books were rare and precious objects, luxurious materials were used: leather, gold, silver, ivory.

Today the role of the cover is more complicated. It now serves to identify the book, to insert it into a style or genre. To embellish it, to make it more effective in the window display of a bookstore. To intrigue passersby so that, once attracted, they come in and pick it up, so that they buy it.

As soon as the book puts on a jacket, the book acquires a new personality. It says something even before being read, just as clothes say something about us before we speak.

A cover elicits certain expectations. It introduces a tone, an attitude, even when these don't fit the book. I have just compared it to a face, but it is also a mask, something that hides what is behind. It can seduce the reader. It can betray him or her. Like gold tinsel, its glitter can deceive.

One might say that it calls into play the opposition between true and false, appearance and reality.

The cover confers on a book not one identity but two. It introduces an expressive element distinct from that of the text. There is what the text says, and what the cover says. That is why one can love the cover and hate the book, or vice versa.

I confess to having bought a book for

its cover more than once, simply because I could not resist it, because I fell under its spell. I trusted the image, even if the content was less convincing. I have a collection of Anchor pocket books with jackets designed by Edward Gorey, an illustrator whose macabre images I have always loved. If I see one in a used bookstore, no matter what the book is, I buy it right away. In this case, I realize, the cover is more valuable to me than the text.

The cover, therefore, has an independent identity. It has a presence, a power of its own.

In Rome, I do not own many books. When we came to Italy, we brought very few with us. Our apartment has a large bookcase, with space for many volumes. It would have been absurd, also sad, to shelve twenty or so books on it. Instead, to fill up the space, I decided to display the books face out. As a consequence, during the past few years, I spend a lot of time enjoying certain covers, aware of the effect they have on me.

Over time the bookcase has become a sort of installation in progress that reflects my reading, my Roman life. A portrait painted by Titian, a snapshot of the poet Patrizia Cavalli, and the photographs of Marco Delogu keep me company. I exhibit the jackets of novels and books of essays by my new Italian friends, as if they were the framed pictures of my new family. In Rome, my books compensate for walls bereft of paintings and other beautiful things. In an apartment rented already furnished, a little devoid of personal effects, the books represent my taste, my presence.

It makes quite an impression to display books with the jacket fronts facing out rather than the spines. Usually, all in a row on a shelf, books are discrete, rather reserved. They form part of the background, reassuring but neutral. Faced-out jackets are, conversely, extroverted, uninhibited, unique. They demand attention. They say: *Look at us*.

3.

Correspondence and Collaboration

Dressing a book is an art, there's no doubt. A published volume sits at the intersection of two forms of creative expression. Every book jacket implies the touch of an artist. And this pairing, this understanding between writer and artist, interests me greatly.

An example that has always struck me is the collaboration between Virginia Woolf and her sister, Vanessa Bell, who designed a series of book covers, now iconic, for almost all of Woolf's first editions with Hogarth Press, in England. This independent publishing house was founded in 1917 specifically to publish books by Woolf; her husband, Leonard; and friends and acquaintances, free from commercial considerations and protected from censorship. At first the books were hand-printed. The printing press sat on the Woolfs' dining table at home.

Bell's covers are powerful, unconventional, modernist. They perfectly express the experimental essence of Woolf's work. And yet, typically, Bell didn't read the whole book. Woolf would recount the plot for her so that she could create a corresponding image. A dialogue between the author and the artist was enough. The critic S. P. Rosenbaum calls the covers "optical echoes" of the texts, citing an expression by Henry James.

As a writer I often search in vain for this "optical echo." I too want my covers to reflect the sense and spirit of my books. I would like it if, even once, a cover for one of my books were designed by someone who knew me well, who deeply knew my work, for whom it really mattered.

I have never spoken with the designers of my covers. I don't know them, I'm not involved. I see the final product, these days as an attachment to an email. I can sign off on it or not, perhaps ask for small changes. I ask myself if the artist has read the book, or one chapter, or even a few pages before designing something. I ask myself if she or he liked the book. It's not clear to me.

Not knowing the person behind the cover, I don't feel free to critique it. The publishing house handles all interactions. They send me the results of the artist's labors, and let the artist know of my reaction. But there's no way to interact directly with the artist. He or she remains a mysterious, hidden figure. A distance remains between us.

Every author has a reaction to his or her covers, but few speak of it openly. A few months ago I came across a brief but pointed text on the subject by the Italian author Lalla Romano. In an essay titled "The Einaudi Covers" ("Le copertine Einaudi"), published in the collection *Un sogno del Nord* (*A Dream of the North*), she analyzes and evaluates the covers of her primary publishing house. She writes: "Because I come from painting, the look of the book is not just an intriguing element but something fundamental. It is very hard to love an ugly book (as object), often all the more ugly because it wants to be *beautiful*." I was struck by her words.

Lullu Romano, like me, searches for the "perfect resonance with the style of the book." She participated, like Woolf, in the decision, suggesting certain images, designs, paintings. From an exchange between author and artist springs the ideal exchange between jacket and text.

We don't live in a world in which a cover can simply reflect the sense and style of the book. Today more than ever the cover shoulders an additional weight. Its function is much more commercial than aesthetic. It succeeds or fails in the market.

In modern mass publishing, a cover contains a lot of information beyond the title of the book, the name of the author, and a design. It lists past awards and honors, quotes from critics and other writers who have liked the book, information pertaining to bestseller lists. It has become a label that lists the ingredients. Sometimes a wraparound band is added, a sort of belt on top of the jacket to indicate, for example, that the book has gone into a second printing, or fourth, or ninth; or to draw to the reader's attention some other "hot" news, information, reviews.

I think that publishers today have overloaded covers with unreasonable expectations. They must grab and win the attention of dazed and disoriented browsers in big bookstores, who must pluck this book and only this one from overstuffed shelves or a table blanketed in volumes. All of the energy and strategy behind a book cover underlines a depressing fact: the terrifying number of books published in the world every year, and the few that are actually bought and read.

Despite the exalted role of the covers, in the end, they don't get much respect. Book jackets are often blamed if a book doesn't sell. I often hear editors say: "The book is beautiful. Too bad the cover was wrong."

To be badly dressed is always a condemnation. But, just as with the wrong clothing, one can take off a book jacket—in the case of a hardcover, quite literally—and put on another. In America, if a first edition doesn't sell well enough, the cover is changed for the paperback edition, and in Italy they do the same. Every once in a while, I'll like a proposed cover, but then the publishing house informs me: "We've decided to go in another direction." The cover remains something removable, interchangeable. Regardless of its power, if it doesn't sell the book, it has no value.

4.

The Naked Book

Let's move in a different direction and speak of the naked book.

I did not own many books as a girl. I would go to the library, where books were often undressed: without jackets or any images. I would find only hardcovers, and the pages that they contained.

I am the daughter of a librarian, and I too worked for many years in the public library where I grew up, from which I used to borrow books. I know that it is costly, also challenging, to protect the covers of volumes that will be read repeatedly by many. Book jackets are easily damaged and, even though there are ways to protect them—with plastic covers, for example—it is always easier to strip them. Hardcovers are made specifically to live in a library, while paperback pocket editions are more temporary.

I have read hundreds of books, almost all the literature of my schooling, without a summary blurb on the flap, without an author photograph. They had an anonymous quality, secretive. They gave nothing away in advance. To understand them, you had to read them.

The authors I loved at the time were embodied only by their words. The naked cover doesn't interfere. My first reading happened outside of time, ignorant of the market, of current events. The part of me that regards book jackets with suspicion seeks to rediscover that experience.

When I purchase a book today, I acquire a range of other things: a picture of the author, biographical information, reviews. All of this complicates matters. It causes confusion. It distracts me. I hate reading the comments on the cover; it is to them that we owe one of the most repugnant words in the English language: *blurb*. Personally, I think it deplorable to place the words and opinions of others on the book jacket. I want the first words read by the reader of my book to be written by me.

Today the relationship between reader and book is far more mediated, with a dozen people buzzing around. We are never alone together, the text and I. I miss the silence, the mystery of the naked book: solitary, without support. It allows one to read in freedom, without previews or introductions. I believe that a naked book, too, can stand on its own feet.

Unfortunately it can't be sold that way. Almost no one wants to buy something unknown, not even a book, without prior information. In some ways today's reader resembles a tourist who, thanks to the guidebooks—this is, thanks to the impact of the book jacket—begins to inform and orient himself before disembarking in an unknown place. Before discovering it, before being there. Before reading.

The bound galleys of my first book published in the United States resembled a naked book to some degree. No image, just essential information. There was something generic rather than individual about them. In the past, when I would go on tour to promote a book, I would read from the bound galleys. When I was forced to use a copy of the actual book, I would remove the jacket. As I have said, the dressed book no longer belongs to me.

Sixteen years ago in America, when my first collection of stories was about to be released, critics and bookstore owners received imageless bound galleys. Why? Perhaps because even the publishing house, at the time, wanted the advance copies to be pristine, without added distractions or noise, hence without a jacket. This seems right.

These days, unfortunately, even the bound galleys contain what to me is superfluous information. The galleys of my last novel list the size of the printing run, my previous prizes and honors, and the titles of my other books. No matter how "essential" it appears, the packaging seems rigged somehow. I thought that the final cover was not there, but leafing through the galley, I came across a reproduction of it on the first page, followed by the flap copy. It was all there, just slightly hidden. There is no escape. For me, there are no more naked books.

5.

Uniformity and Anarchy

In Italy, I have gotten to know another type of book cover: that which belongs to an editorial series. These covers, so different from American designs, have a powerful effect on me. I find their simplicity and seriousness admirable. They seduce me, just as my cousins' school uniforms did.

The covers that form part of a series are sober, at once generic and immediately recognizable. By now, in an Italian bookshop or at a friend's house, I recognize straightaway the white books belonging to Struzzi Einaudi, the mellow colors of the Adelphi series, the dark blue of Sellerio.

At the moment I am reading two books, both published by Adelphi: *La Pelle* (*The Skin*) by Curzio Malaparte, and *L'Inconveniente di essere nati* (*The Trouble with Being Born*) by Emil Cioran. They are two very different writers but, dressed in Adelphi jackets, the two books resemble each other, as if they were members of the same family, of the same bloodline. The books share the same size and, most important, are products of the same aesthetic sensibility. Both covers bear a framed image, then the title of the book and the name of the author. They are printed on fine paper, which is glued to the book only at the back. I like the fact that the rest of the jacket can be removed from the bound pages, like a tent, and that beneath this light sheet of paper there is a firmer undercover in white. Behold, the naked book.

An editorial series is a system for organizing a large number of books. A library arranged this way is visually harmonious. The husband of an Italian friend of mine orders his bookcases by series, in chromatic order. The effect is marvelous. According to his wife, however, aesthetic virtues aside, it's not a good system. Beautiful to look at, she says, but one can't find anything.

On my desk in Rome I have a row of books from Adelphi's Piccola Biblioteca series. In the mess of my work surface they form an elegant, reassuring island. I own seven. Each bears a number on its spine. When I look at them I feel the need to own the whole series, starting with number one, even though there are more than six hundred.

In my bathroom in Brooklyn, meanwhile, I have grouped, in small frames on the wall, a number of postcards that reproduce covers from the early years of the original Penguin paperback series launched by Allen Lane in 1935: Shakespeare, Agatha Christie, Iris Murdoch, R. D. Laing. These distinctive images have by now come to adorn T-shirts and coffee mugs. Their insignia is tantamount to a literary badge of honor. In high school and in college, reading an orange-spined Penguin Classic felt reassuring, virtuous. I assumed they were works of quality, of substance.

The authors published in the series belong to one another, and they all belong to the publishing house. Each book represents the choice, the taste of the editor, but the series confers on the book an identity, a sort of citizenship. A series says to its authors: *You are one of us.*

This raises an interesting and much debated question. Is the series more important, or the individual books within? I have not yet made up my mind. The series serves the individual text, and also vice versa. On the one hand, the series seems to me a discreet wrapper, less invasive than a wholly unique book cover. On the other, it has a somewhat formal, even pompous, effect.

I think of each editorial series as an exclusive world, a sort of closed circle. I wonder, How does one get in? And yet, at least in Italy, and in England in the case of the original Penguin paperbacks, the editorial series include contemporary authors.

Adelphi's Piccola Biblioteca includes Friedrich Nietzsche and Yasmina Reza, Benedetto Croce and Jamaica Kincaid. In Europe an editorial series is not something musty. On the contrary, I find it can comprise a community, current, international, eclectic, alive.

And yet, an editorial series is also classic, trusted, unchanging. Its value is its continuity, with subtle changes. The uniform vigorously resists fashion, confusion, instability. It exists, something like the naked book, outside time.

I write these words in a library in Rome. It is a magnificent Italian palazzo filled, nonetheless, mostly with American books. I believe I was destined to have discovered it. Here is where I, an anglophone writer, dreamt up and wrote my first book in Italian.

I am surrounded in this library by my past. I think of my father's long life as a librarian, of the library I went to as a girl, of all the librar ies I have frequented and loved in America.

And yet I think and write, here, in Italian. It is here that my writing has taken a new direction.

As I write in Italian, I look up from time to time, to gaze at the books that keep me company. I see the rows of spines. They are organized according to a precise classification. What is lacking, however, is a visual order. I see a jumble of jacketless books, with hard plain covers or protective plastic jackets.

There are books from different ages, different genres, some published recently, some more than a century ago. One sees an amalgam of styles, diversity of thought. One sees little uniformity. There is visual confusion, but also a sort of joyful exuberance. It reminds me of a motley crew, a party made of odd individuals who enjoy one another's company.

It is an inclusive environment. It suggests that any book can join in and take up residence on a shelf. The books belong to the collective and, at the same time, belong only to themselves. Needless to say, American book jackets reflect the spirit of country—little homogeneity, lots of diversity.

If I rise to stretch for a moment, I spot an American editorial series here and there—a set of biographies, or one book in several tomes. Only in this context, books that wear uniforms are the exception, not the rule.

The volumes of an American editorial series—the highly regarded Modern Library, the Library of America—convey that they are classics. The series is an homage to praiseworthy and by now untouchable authors. Uniformity, in this case, is a sign of belonging to the literary canon: unchanging clothes for timeless words.

Jackets of this kind are a strong recognition, a sort of prize, almost always conferred posthumously. Nine out of ten times, the author is dead. A contemporary book by a young author would not be worthy. Unlike the European series, where living and dead authors coexist, the American series seems to me almost a mausoleum.

6.

My Jackets

My books tell stories, but what stories, meanwhile, do my covers tell?

Upon close inspection, my covers tend perfectly to mirror my own double identity, bifurcated, disputed. As a result they are often projections, conjectures.

All my life I have been in conflict between two different identities, both imposed. No matter how I try to free myself from this conflict, I find myself, as a writer, caught in the same trap.

For some publishing houses, my name and photograph are enough to quickly commission a cover that teems with stereotyped references to India: elephants, exotic flowers, henna-painted hands, the Ganges, religious and spiritual symbols. No one considers that the greater part of my stories are set in the United States, and therefore pretty far from the river Ganges.

Once, after I complained that the cover of a book in which the protagonist was born and raised in the United States seemed too "exotic," that a less "oriental" approach was better suited, the publisher removed the image of an enchanting Indian building and replaced it with an American flag. From one stereotype, that is, to another.

For me, therefore, a wrong jacket is not just an aesthetic issue, because it retriggers a series of anxieties felt ever since I was a child. Who am I? How am I seen, dressed, perceived, read? I write not only to avoid the question, but also to seek the answer.

I have the good fortune to have been translated into several foreign languages. Given that I am now the author of five books, I would guess that this means, in all, around one hundred different book covers. One hundred different interpretations.

If I place the different jackets of just one of my books all in a row, it becomes obvious how they change in tone, spirit, identity. I see a lively one, a gloomy one, a bright one. I see birds of various kinds. I see designs, both intricate and minimalist. I see a jacket with just the title, my name, and nothing else. I see explicit allusions to the political aspects of the novel—guns, the hammer and sickle. I see landscapes that evoke Calcutta, and I see a bunch of flowers on a table. I see two boys who are diving into water.

On the one hand, it is lovely to see them together, to take in the abundance of styles, the variety. On the other, I ask myself: How is it possible that one book, the same book, can generate this panorama of images? All of these covers have been inspired by the same story. Translations notwithstanding, every sentence is the same. And yet they seem like twelve different books, with twelve diverging themes, written by twelve different authors.

The differences also reflect each nation's identity and collective taste. It is very rare for the editor of my book in one country to like the book jacket of another. They usually say, politely, "how interesting," then add that it would never work in their country, for their readers. A cover that one person cherishes is devoid of meaning to another. What does this mean? I fear that, even in a globalized world, it signals an inability to recognize oneself in the other.

Like the language in which the text is written, the book jacket can constitute a barrier. During the period in which I was writing this essay, I found myself in a bookstore in Holland. The books all around me were in Dutch, a language in which I can't read a word. It made no sense to open any of the books and glance at the first page. As I looked at the books, I could take in only their visual impact. They remained objects to me, as if the bookstore were a museum in which one could look but not buy. I found the covers attractive, but mostly, I found them foreign. I quickly realized, in the Amsterdam bookstore, that I was somewhere else. Each country's jackets form a distinct geography, an unmistakable landscape.

Everyone likes to judge a book cover. In the first place, it is easier to evaluate the cover than the content. Besides, it's fun. All one needs to do is look and react. I'd like to share some of the comments by friends in Italy to draft versions of the American and British jackets for my last novel, *The Lowland*:

It looks like a cookie tin.
It reminds me of an adventure book
    for adolescents.
It looks like a Persian carpet.
It seems like a political thriller.
Looks like a book written by the pope.

My latest book, *In altre parole* (*In Other Words*), is written in Italian. Its arrival introduces a new and unexpected element in my literary identity. It speaks of the Italian language, and my relationship to it. It does not share much with the books that preceded it. It is a meditative book, autobiographical, without much of a setting.

The first cover, the Italian one, is one that I like. It shows a woman seen from the back, facing a sort of wall. And yet the image is light, open, ambiguous. It communicates, I think, the sense of my literary project, even though I never spoke with the illustrator. I didn't expect it, it came as a surprise, but I consider it nevertheless the right cover for this book. In this case, the adventure has a happy ending.

In altre parole is being translated into

various languages and, during this period, I am asked to evaluate one book cover after another. The UK and the American editions have a picture of me in a library in Rome. The Dutch edition has another photo of me, in close-up and out of focus. They think that it conveys the personal and introspective nature of the book. The French bears no image at all.

My first reaction to the idea of having my picture on the cover was negative. I was afraid that it would be judged as an act of vanity, a brazen way to market a niche book. I later reconsidered.

Both photos of me were taken by Marco Delogu, someone who knows me, who has read my books, someone I trust. Together we chose both portraits. Before he took the shot in the library, we talked about it. I told him what I wanted and he listened to me. Thus, for the first time, I was able to participate in the creation of a book jacket. In the end the author is the book, and represents the work directly, also sincerely. Better a photo of me than an annoying, irrelevant image. Maybe it makes sense that, in America, in England, in Holland, I have become my own cover.

Even when I don't particularly like one of my jackets, I end up feeling some affinity for it. Over time, the covers become a part of me, and I identify with them. Recently, in Italy, a peculiar thing happened: I was sent a complimentary book by an Italian publisher, and this book—the Italian edition of a novel written in English by a writer of Indian origin—has the same cover as the current American edition of my first book of short stories. It is identical in every detail.

Opening the envelope, taking it in, I was

dumbfounded. At first I thought that it was my own book, but then I realized that it had more pages and that the title and the author's name were different. I quickly called my agent. "But this is my jacket!" I told her. Apparently such things can happen. In any case it's too late, the fat twin to my book is already out. The other day at the Rome airport I came across a stack of them, believing for a second that they were mine.

Years ago, I thought that that cover had been made to measure. I thought that it would belong to my book, only mine, and that it would remain faithful to me. Instead, the same jacket that dressed my words has since abandoned me for another author, in another country, without, however, leaving me altogether.

7.

The Living Jacket, the Dead Jacket, the Perfect Jacket

Today, the printed book is no longer the only manifestation of a published text. What is the significance of the cover when there is no longer a physical volume? I don't read e-books, but I don't think that jackets have the same function, the same presence, on a screen. Strangely, the screen privileges the text, and the graphic garment no longer dresses or protects. It remains a detail, an accessory, an element that is ancillary and, I would say, gratuitous. It becomes even more of a label. A paper cover, over time, gets dirty, gets ruined. On the screen, nothing of the kind takes place.

An American painter I know and admire, Richard Baker, has for many years dedicated a series of paintings to classic book covers. He usually selects, as his models, pocket editions, that is, the most modest and inexpensive of editions (among his subjects are several of the original Penguin paperbacks). Many are books that have changed his life. The paintings resemble hyperrealistic gouache photographs. Baker depicts the books faithfully, with affection but with an unsparing eye. He ingeniously copies, and also transfigures, the graphic designs of others.

All of the books have been lived with,

held in hand day after day. Their covers are tattered, yellowed, bleached by the sun. It is as if they were faces, furrowed, worn. They are, through and through, alive.

Each one of Baker's paintings is the portrait of a book, but they tell us much more. They recount the passion of reading, both Baker's and all of ours. They narrate the literary education of a generation. They preserve on canvas a world, a culture that is declining. They elicit nostalgia, recalling an era that no longer exists. Above all they show the relationship, the strong ties of affection, almost a fusion, between reader and book. Baker has said that books "come to stand for various episodes in our lives, for certain idealisms, follies of belief, moments of love. Along the way they accumulate our marks, our stains, our innocent abuses—they come to wear our

experience of them on their covers and bind-
ings like wrinkles on our skin."

By immortalizing the book covers of his
life, Baker depicts how they age and, in the
end, die, like we do. They express something
fleeting, never definite, never permanent.

What is the perfect book jacket? It doesn't
exist. The great majority of covers, like our
clothes, don't last forever. They make sense,
give pleasure, in only a specific arc of time,
after which they are dated. Over the years
they need redesign, change, just like old translations. A new jacket is given to a book to
reinvigorate it, to make it more current. The
only part left intact is the original text, in the
language in which it was written.

Like Richard Baker, I remain faithful to the
book covers that have changed my life. If I see
an edition of Joyce's *Portrait of the Artist as a*

Young Man or Shakespeare's *Complete Works* other than the one I read in college, it seems like a different book. I fear that the unknown edition, the one I did not hold, that did not accompany me to the library, that I did not mark up and study, that I did not fall in love with, would not elicit the same emotion in me.

I remain attached even to certain ugly covers of books I would read and return in high school without ever owning them. In the end, the beauty of the cover has nothing to do with it. Like every true love, that of the reader is blind.

If it were possible for me to choose one of my covers, how would I choose? The uniform jacket of an editorial series? Or something original created specifically for my book?

On the one hand, I want desperately to belong, to have a clear identity. On the other, I refuse to belong, and I believe that my hybrid identity enriches me. I will probably always remain torn between these two roads, these two impulses.

I would certainly prefer the uniformed elegance of a series to an insipid cover, or one that pains me. And yet I know that expressing oneself necessarily means being different. The writer's voice is a singular one, solitary. Art is nothing other than the freedom to express oneself in any language, in whatever manner, dressed any which way.

If I could dress a book myself, I would like a still life by Morandi on the cover, or maybe a collage by Matisse. It would make no commercial sense, and would probably not mean anything to the reader. But I recognize myself in the abstract eye, the chromatic palette, the language of each of these painters. It would make sense to me.

I wrote this last sentence one evening. The following morning, after I'd stated my wish, something marvelous happened. Right in front of the gate to the building where I live in Rome there is a bus stop with two signposts close together.

By lovely coincidence, as I was writing this speech, Rome was host to two exhibits: Morandi and Matisse. When I exited my building the following morning, looking up, I saw, on the signpost to my right, a poster of a still life by Morandi, and to my left, a work by Matisse. For a few moments I stood between them and, imagining myself transformed into the pages of a book, I was jacketed by both.

Afterword

In 2014, while on holiday in Capalbio, Italy, I received a call from Beatrice Monti della Corte—cofounder, along with her late husband, Gregor von Rezzori, of the Santa Maddalena Foundation—inviting me to deliver the *lectio magistralis*, the keynote speech, for the ninth edition of the Festival degli Scrittori in Florence the following spring. The theme of the speech was open, though it should have something to do with writing, Beatrice said. I accepted her proposal gladly, but also with some trepidation, recalling the eloquent *lectio* that Carlos Fuentes had delivered some years back, which I'd had the pleasure and privilege of hearing in person.

On a train that autumn, talking to my friend Sara Antonelli, a professor of American literature in Rome and a translator into Italian of some of my most beloved authors, including Nathaniel Hawthorne and Thomas Hardy, I pondered topics for my speech. I considered writing about the significance of titles: a title, after all, is the first element of a book one encounters, something that both represents and stands apart from the text.

"What about covers?" Sara suggested, taking this idea a step further and into a different kind of language—the visual. I was immediately inspired, and as we kept talking I began taking notes on the journey between Florence and Rome.

I wrote this essay, originally titled "Il vestito dei libri," in Rome, in Italian. It was first edited by Sara, then by Michela Gallio, an editor whom I met through my Italian publisher, Guanda, and with whom I have worked closely on various projects. It was translated into English by my husband, Alberto Vourvoulias-Bush, and then the Italian text and the English translation were published together as a chapbook by the Santa Maddalena Foundation, with the invaluable assistance of Brigida Beccari, for the occasion of the festival. I presented it, in Italian, in the Cenacolo di Santa Croce on the evening of June 10, 2015.

The following June, in the United States, I revisited both texts in order to prepare the

English translation for publication. Back in Rome, after slightly modifying the translation, after correcting a couple of mistakes and adding one or two new thoughts, I had to rework the Italian text, translating myself, this time from English, in order to arrive at the final version. I'm struck by this repeated crossing between the two languages in which I write. I realize how useful it is to move back and forth linguistically. I also realize that the process is endless and that, as a result, the final version continues to elude me.

The bilingual edition published by the Santa Maddalena Foundation exemplifies the naked book I talk about. The cover—stark, cream-colored—bears only the title of my address and my name, without any design other than the emblem of the festival it belonged to. It is part of a small, exclusive series. Now that original book with two languages inside will become two separate volumes, each containing a single language. The American edition will wear its cover, the Italian another. The journey of this little book—born as a double text wearing a neutral uniform, then split in two, dressed in two separate garments—seems right.

I am grateful to Alberto for rendering this essay into English, and to Robin Desser, my editor at Knopf, for publishing it in its current form.

About the Author

Jhumpa Lahiri is the author of four works of fiction: *Interpreter of Maladies*, *The Namesake*, *Unaccustomed Earth*, and *The Lowland*; and a work of nonfiction, *In Other Words*. She has received numerous awards, including the Pulitzer Prize; the PEN/Hemingway Award; the Frank O'Connor International Short Story Award; the Premio Gregor von

Rezzori; the DSC Prize for South Asian Literature; a 2014 National Humanities Medal, awarded by President Barack Obama; and the Premio Internazionale Viareggio-Versilia, for *In altre parole*.